With Lo from Mom

Bobbie Wolgemuth

HB
HONOR
BOOKS

08 07 06 05 04 03   10 9 8 7 6 5 4 3 2 1

With Love from Mom
ISBN 1-56292-759 0

Copyright by Barbara J. Wolgemuth

Published by Honor Books
An imprint of Cook Communications Ministries
P. O. Box 55388
Tulsa, Oklahoma 74155

Dear friend and fellow mom,

Mothers love their children. That's for sure. But getting children to feel just how much they are loved may take an extra effort. Two sure ways to let them know that they are important and loved like crazy is to stay in touch and to do it in writing. Your child's love cup is never too full. Here are some special ways to let the most important young people in your life know how important they are.

These tear-out notes are organized so you can match them to exactly what's happening between you and your child. You can include them with a letter, hand them out before they climb onto the school bus, or plant them in their lunch boxes. Whether you tape one to a mirror or lay one on their bed pillow, they'll get the message.

My sincere hope is that these notes will give you another chance to let your children know how important they are to you and how very much they are loved.

God Bless You,

Bobbie Wolgemuth

Follow the steps below to turn these pages into special notes from you to your kids.

1 Remove a note from the book.

Personalize it in any way you wish. **2**

3 Fold the note as shown.

Seal it with a sticker from the back of the book.

4

5 Give the note to your daughter or tuck it in a letter or someplace special as a surprise.

With Love
from Mom

There are millions
of children in the world,
but I am thankful that
YOU are my child!
I love you so much.

For:

Your life is full of beauty, both
on the inside and the outside.
I admire your tender heart.
Have a wonderful day.

For:

*W*hen I think I could never love you more than I already do, I find myself loving you even more. I'm so glad you're mine.

For:

*W*hen I think of your smile,
it makes me happy.
Your happiness brightens my day.
You are my sunshine.

I LOVE YOU

For:

Being with you brings me such joy. You make even dark or rainy days happy. You lighten up the room.

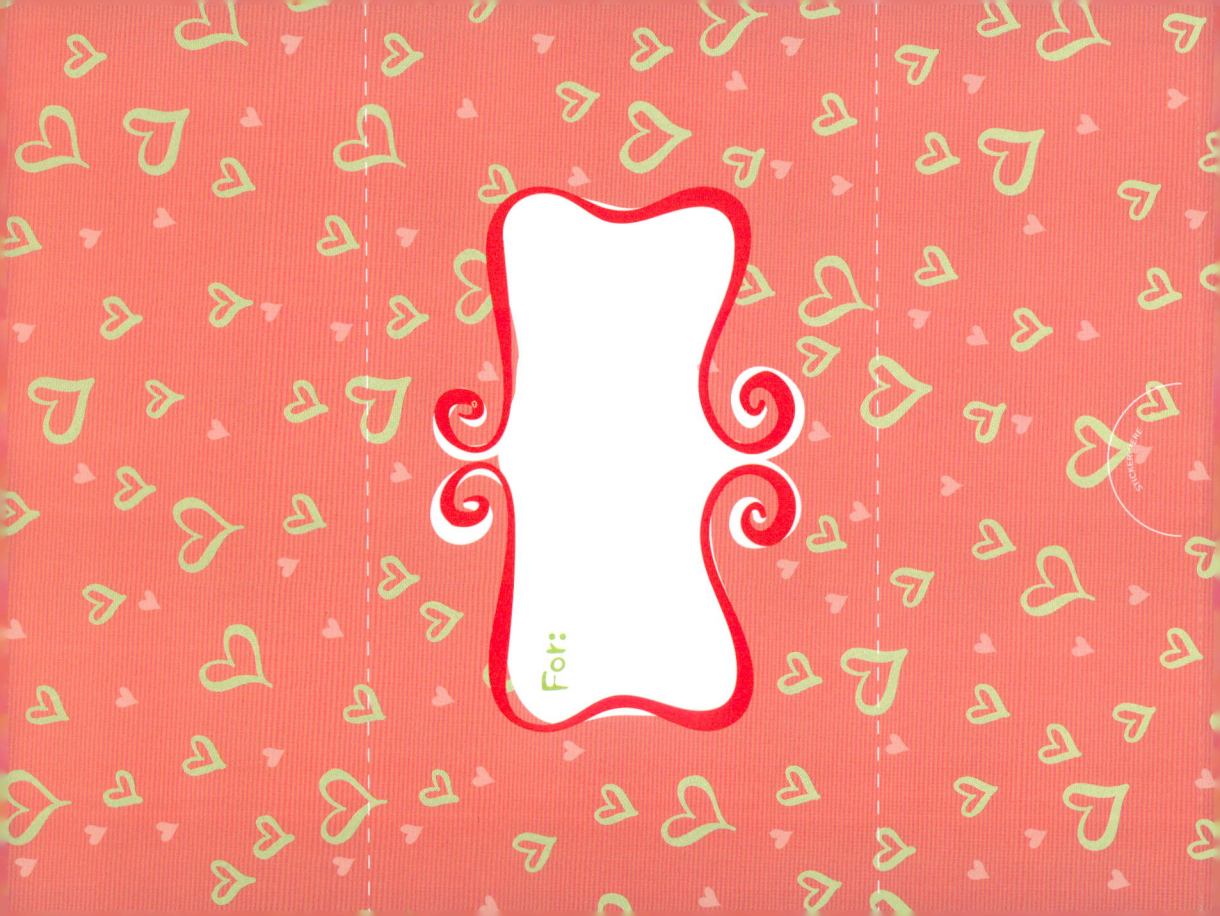

For:

No matter what happens to you and me, no matter where we are, you will always be my precious child. I love you so much.

For:

What could be more wonderful than knowing my child loves me? I am the luckiest lady in town! That's for sure.

For:

There is nothing quite as wonderful as having a special friend like you.
I love you like crazy!

For:

What could be more wonderful
than knowing my child loves me?
I am the luckiest lady in town!
That's for sure.

For:

When I see you helping around the house, it makes me realize how responsible you are. I appreciate your effort.

For:

Thank you for your gift to me.
It will always remind me of
how special you are.
This "thank you" comes
with a smile and a hug!

For:

STICKER HERE

Even though I'm a busy grown-up,
it makes me feel so warm and
happy to remember that
you love me like you do.
I will always cherish you.

For:

STICKER HERE

Sometimes I forget to stop and notice beautiful things. You help me to see God's beauty everywhere.
Thank you for that.

For:

Friends are one of God's greatest gifts.
I am so glad that you are
one of my best friends.
I value our relationship.

For:

You listen so well. It's so easy and
so much fun to talk to you.
I'm glad I have you in my life.

For:

Your smile is contagious.
When you smile, it helps me
remember to enjoy life.
Thank you for spreading joy
to others—especially me!

For:

Thank you for being so obedient.
And thank you for doing it
with a smile on your face.
That means so much to me.

For:

I am sorry that I made you sad by what I said. I'm sorry. I was wrong. Will you please forgive me?

For:

I forgot. I know that I should have remembered, but I didn't. I'm sorry. That must have hurt your feelings. Please forgive me.

For:

When you were talking to me, I wasn't listening. I know that hurt your feelings. I'm sorry for being so insensitive. I'm working on being a good listener, and I need your forgiveness.

For:

I would never hurt your feelings on purpose, but I know that I did hurt you. That makes me feel terrible, and I need you to forgive me.

For:

I am sorry that you were left out. I should have included you. I'm sorry. That wasn't very caring and I was wrong. Will you please forgive me?

For:

I should have known better than to do what I did. I'm sorry. I want to be the kind of mom you can trust. Will you please forgive me?

For:

Sometimes I am in too much of a hurry, and I need to slow down. Will you help me to be aware of that? Please forgive me for rushing.

For:

You are doing so well.
Your hard work
has really paid off.
You really amaze me!

For:

Thank you for your excellent manners. You behaved very well. You sure do set the standard.

For:

You show your love for God
in such a winsome way.
Your actions reveal a heart
that is honest and pure.
I admire you and love you so much.

For:

I'm so proud of you for
choosing good friends.
I like it when you bring them over
to our house. I love having all of
you around—especially you!

For:

I notice the way you take such good care of your things. You are taking responsibility and that means a lot to me. I appreciate your effort and am so proud of you.

For:

Sometimes things don't turn out the way we wished they would. But you gave it your very best, and that's a very good thing. You handled it all like the treasure you are.

For:

I'm so proud of you. Doing
well in school is very important,
and I know you're working
very hard to do your best.
Thanks for the incredible effort.
I love you so much.

For:

I'm so proud of you
for showing kindness to others.
You set a wonderful example
for others to follow.
I love you so much.

For:

How does the cow put on her shoes? First, she puts on one, and then the udder.
I love to make you smile.

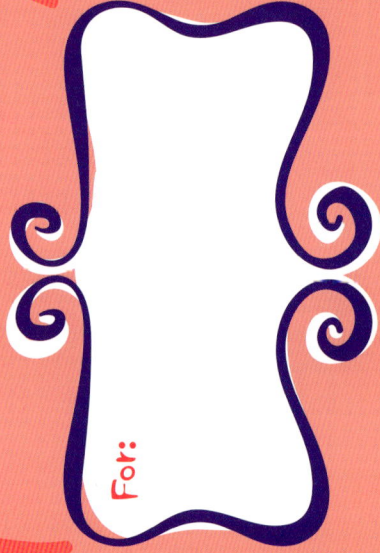

For:

What is a knight's
favorite fish?
A swordfish!
I love when you laugh.

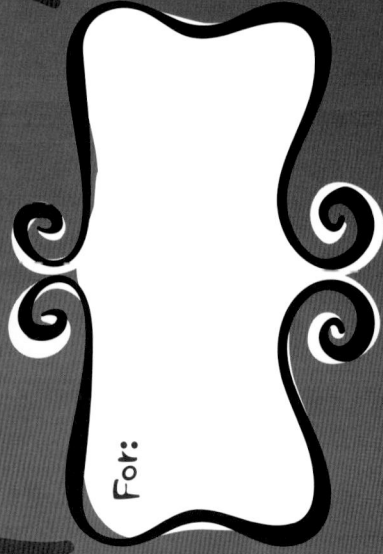

For:

What did the spider eat for lunch? He had a hamburger and flies. Did I make you smile?

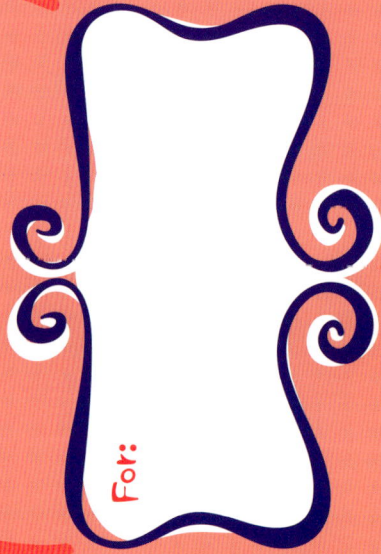

For:

*W*hat does a cow sing?
She sings silly "Moo-sic."
I love when you smile.

For:

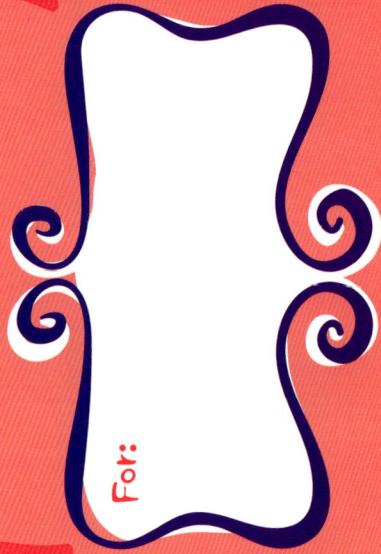
STICKER HERE

What kind of snake
builds houses?
A boa-constructor.
Did you laugh?

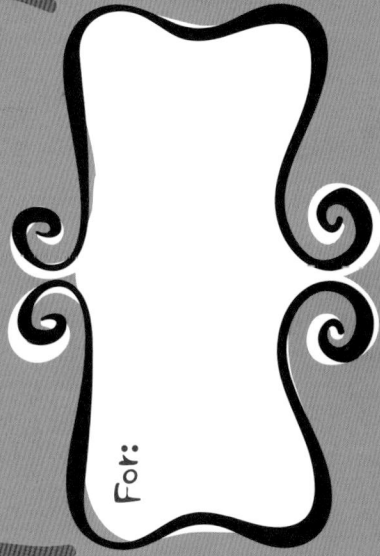

For:

*W*hy are frogs so happy?
Because they eat whatever
"bugs" them!
This is one of my favorites. Smile!

For:

*W*hy didn't Santa leave
any gifts for the little beaver?
Because he was so
"gnaw-ty" all year long.
I love to make you laugh.

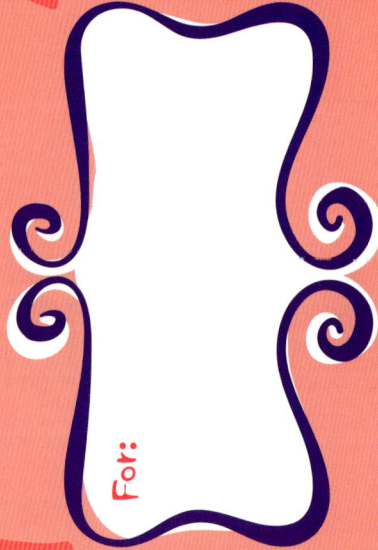

For:

You are working very
hard at school, and
doing your best.
I want you to know
I'm praying for you.

For:

Don't worry about
anything . . . Tell God
what you need, and
thank him for all he has done.

PHILIPPIANS 4:6 NLT

For:

Friends are such an
important part of your life.
I hope you will choose wisely
whom you will spend time with.
You can be sure that I'm praying
for you every day.

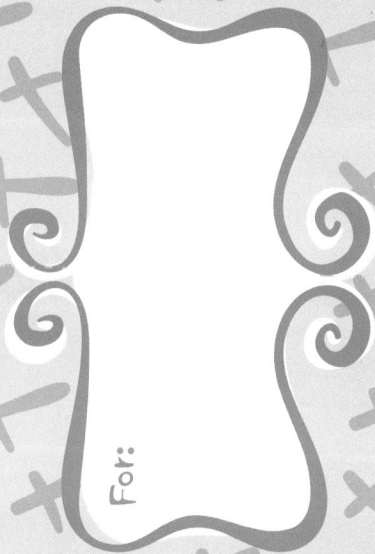

For:

He who walks with
the wise grows wise.

Proverbs 13:20 niv

For:

I'm sad when I see you hurt by people who are mean to you. I want you to know that I'm praying that God will heal your heart and help you to stay loving.

For:

This is a time when you are making important decisions. I know that you want to make the right choices, so I want you to know that you have someone praying for you—me.

For:

Remember the Lord in everything you do, and he will show you the right way.

Proverbs 3:6 GNB

For:

Being sick is no fun at all.
I want you to get better
very soon. Just know that
I'm praying for you today.

For:

He heals me.

PSALM 103:3 TLB

For:

The most important thing in the whole world is to love God and know how very much He loves you. I want you to know that I love you, too, and am praying for you.

For:

The Father loves us.
He loves us so much
that he lets us be
called his children.

1 JOHN 3:1 CEV

I'M PRAYING FOR YOU

For:

The good thing about making mistakes is that we can learn lessons from them.
I hope you will be stronger because of what happened. I'm praying for you.

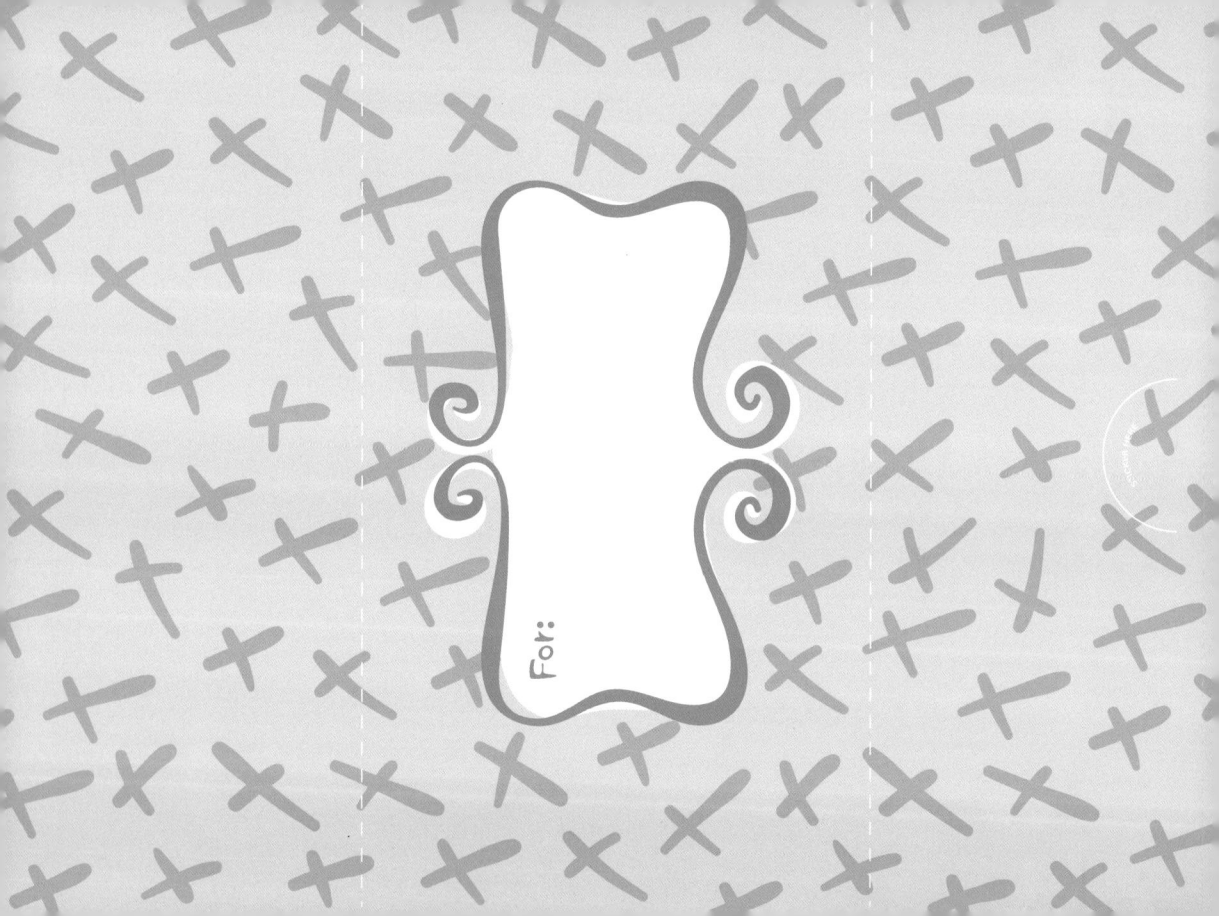

For:

God has forgiven you through Christ.

EPHESIANS 4:32 GNB

I'M PRAYING FOR YOU

For:

*W*hen I'm away from you,
I miss seeing your face.
I'll just have to close my eyes and
picture you until I can be with you.

For:

When I'm away from you,
I miss hearing you laugh.
I can't wait to come home
to be with you.

For:

STICKER HERE

When I'm away from you,
I miss our time to say prayers together.
We can still pray for each other
while we're apart. Soon I'll be home.

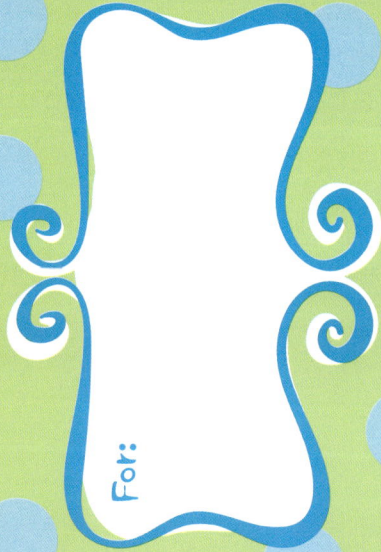

For:

When I'm away from you, I miss seeing your happy face in the morning. I miss eating breakfast together. Let's have a crunchy bowl of cereal together when I get back.

For:

STICKER HERE

When I'm away from you, I miss the fun we have playing games together. I love to laugh, even if you win the game. I can't wait to come home to be with you.

For:

*W*hen I'm away from you,
I miss listening to your voice.
You have so many wonderful things to say.
I can't wait to come home to be with you.

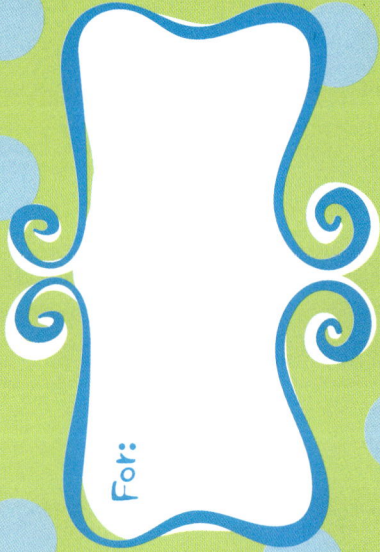

For:

*W*hen I'm away from you
I really miss your smile and
the way you always make me smile.
I can't wait to hear about your day.

For:

About the Author

Bobbie Wolgemuth has been in the mothering business for more than 31 years. She has reared two daughters to adulthood and has been involved in various ministries including Campus Life, Bethany Christian Services, and The Foundation. She has been a guest on Focus on the Family broadcasts on numerous occasions relating to parenting, music, and marriage.

She recently co-authored with Joni Eareckson Tada, John MacArthur, and her husband Robert a four-book/CD series, Great Hymns of Our Faith (Crossway), which highlight stories and recorded hymns for use in personal devotions. The first book, entitled O Worship the King, was a best-seller. Bobbie is also the co-author of The Most Important Year of a Woman's Life: What every groom wished his bride knew about the first year of marriage (Zondervan, Spring 2003) and Hymns for a Kid's Heart (Focus on the Family/Crossway, Summer 2003) with Joni Eareckson Tada.

Bobbie and her husband Robert have two adult daughters, two sons-in-law, and three grandchildren. They live in central Florida.

Additional copies of this book are available from your local bookstore.

If you have enjoyed this book, or it has
impacted your life, we would like to hear from you.
Please contact us at:

Honor Books
Department E
P.O. Box 55388
Tulsa, Oklahoma 74155
Or by e-mail at info@honorbooks.com.

Honor Books